EASY PIANO

LAUREN DAIGLE
LOOK UP CHILD

ISBN 978-1-5400-4595-9

Visit Hal Leonard Online at
www.halleonard.com

Contact us:
Hal Leonard
7777 West Bluemound Road
Milwaukee, WI 53213
Email: info@halleonard.com

In Europe, contact:
Hal Leonard Europe Limited
42 Wigmore Street
Marylebone, London, W1U 2RN
Email: info@halleonardeurope.com

In Australia, contact:
Hal Leonard Australia Pty. Ltd.
4 Lentara Court
Cheltenham, Victoria, 3192 Australia
Email: info@halleonard.com.au

CONTENTS

STILL ROLLING STONES

Words and Music by LAUREN DAIGLE,
PAUL DUNCAN, JASON INGRAM
and PAUL MABURY

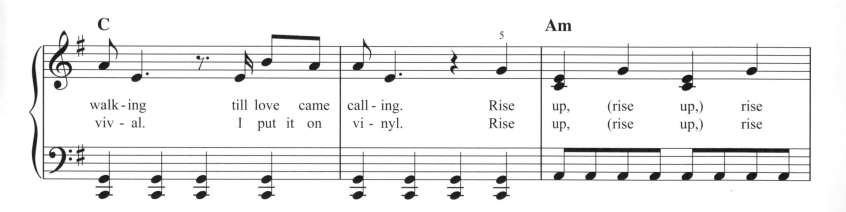

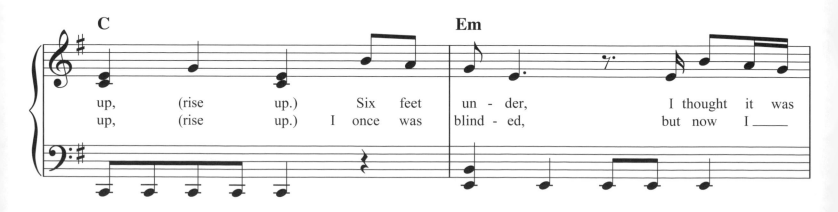

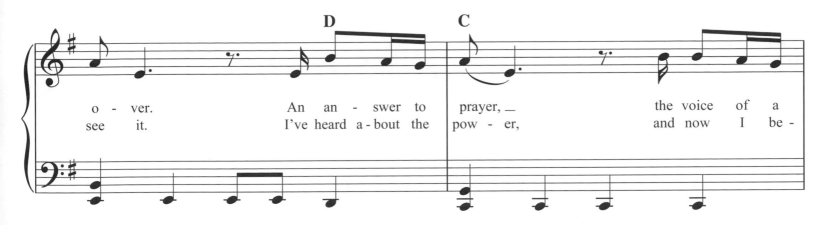

C(add2)

Yeah, I'm the one who dug this grave, but You called

1.

Am   B7

my name, You called my name.

2.

Am   C   B7

my name, You called my name.

Em   C   D   Bm   Em   C

All at once I came a - live. This beat - ing heart, these o -

-pen eyes.__ The grave __ let go.__ The dark - ness should _ have

known. _____ You're still roll - ing stones. _____

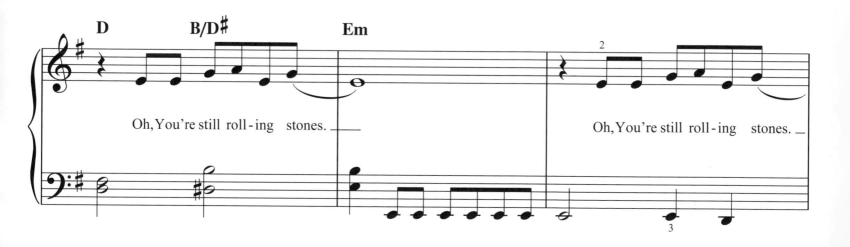

Oh, You're still roll - ing stones. _____ Oh, You're still roll - ing stones.__

_____ Oh, You're still roll - ing stones. __ You're still roll - ing, roll - ing.__

You're still roll - ing, roll - ing. ___ You're still roll - ing stones. ___

Much slower, freely

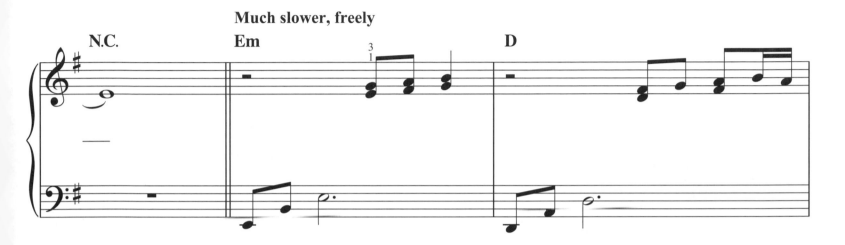

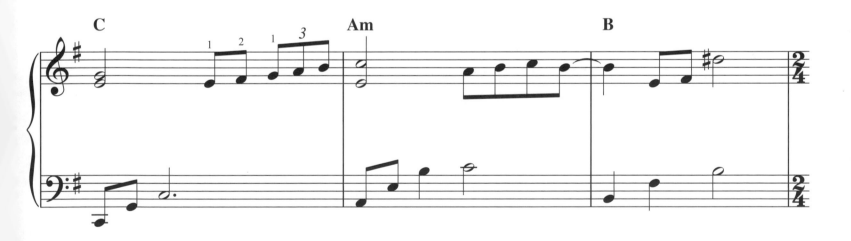

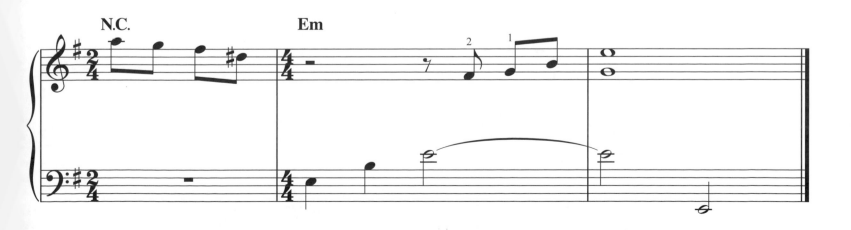

RESCUE

Words and Music by LAUREN DAIGLE,
JASON INGRAM and PAUL MABURY

Moderately slow, in 2

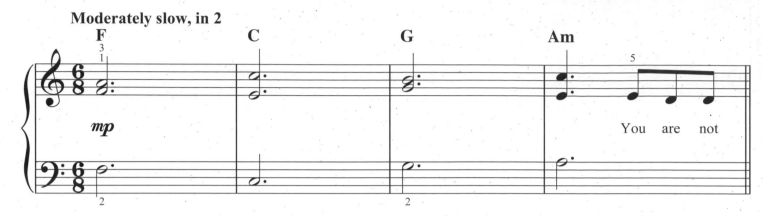

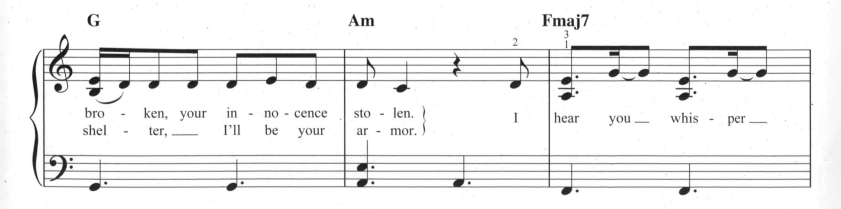

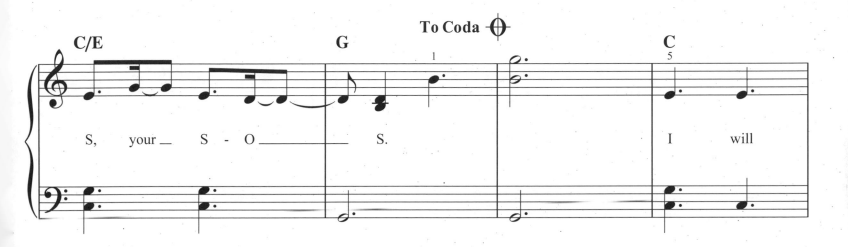

CODA

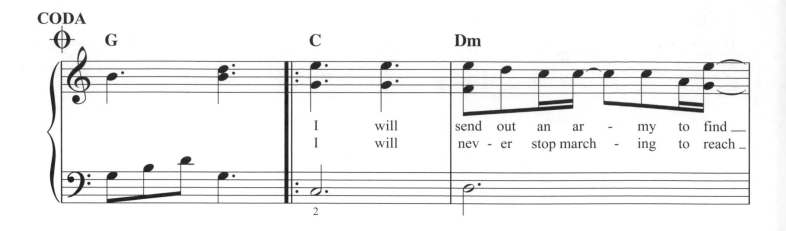

I will send out an ar - my to find __
I will nev - er stop march - ing to reach __

__ you in the mid - dle of the dark - est night, it's true.
__ you in the mid - dle of the hard - est fight, it's true.

I will __ res - cue __

__ you. __

1.
F(add2)

2.
Fmaj7

I hear the __ whis - per __

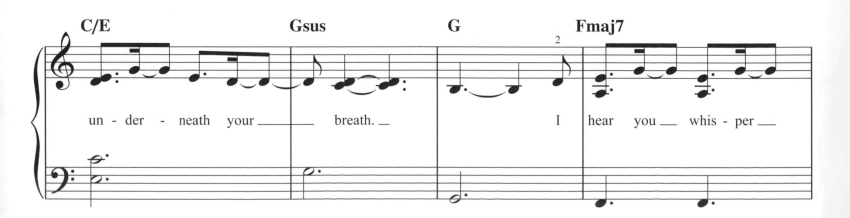

un - der - neath your __ breath. __

I hear you __ whis - per __

13

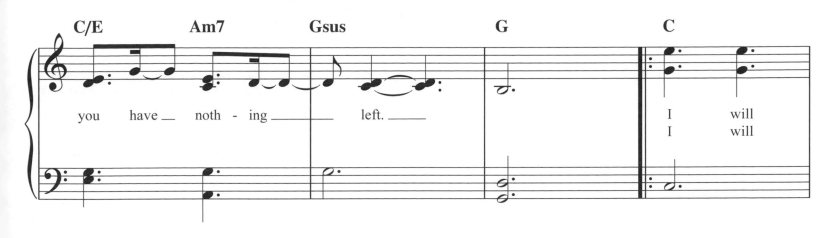

you have — noth - ing — left. — I will
I will

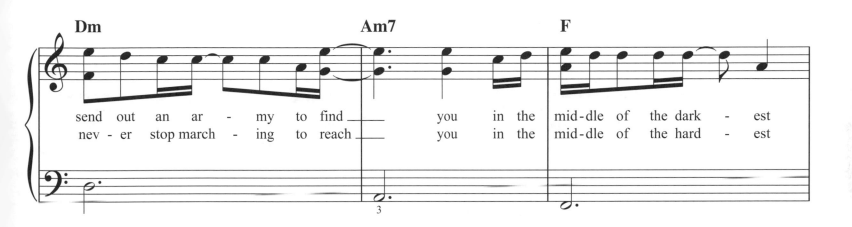

send out an ar - my to find — you in the mid-dle of the dark - est
nev - er stop march - ing to reach — you in the mid-dle of the hard - est

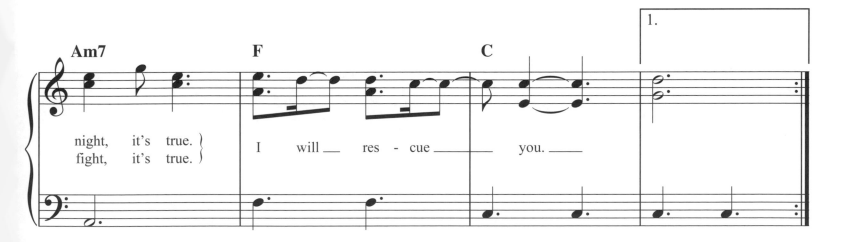

1.

night, it's true. I will — res - cue — you. —
fight, it's true.

2.

Oh, — I will — res - cue — you. —

LOVE LIKE THIS

Words and Music by LAUREN DAIGLE,
JASON INGRAM and PAUL MABURY

When I ___ am a waste - land,
When I ___ am a long ___ night,
Your voice ___ like a whis - per,

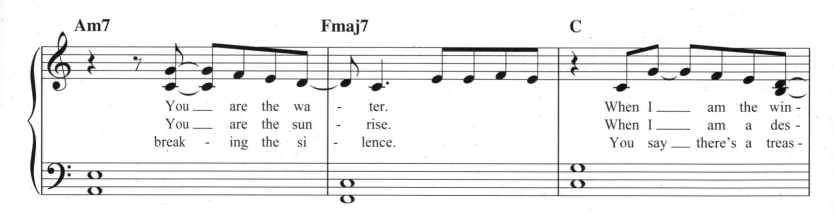

You ___ are the wa - ter.
You ___ are the sun - rise.
break - ing the si - lence.

When I ___ am the win -
When I ___ am a des -
You say ___ there's a treas -

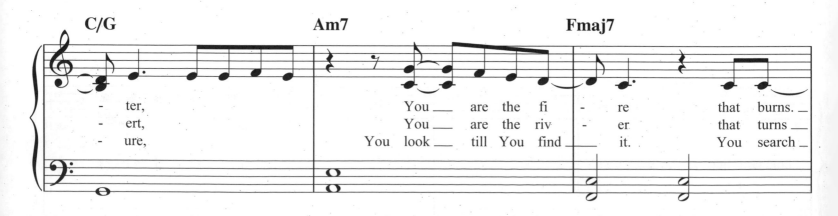

- ter,
- ert,
- ure,

You ___ are the fi - re that burns.
You ___ are the riv - er that turns ___
You look ___ till You find ___ it. You search ___

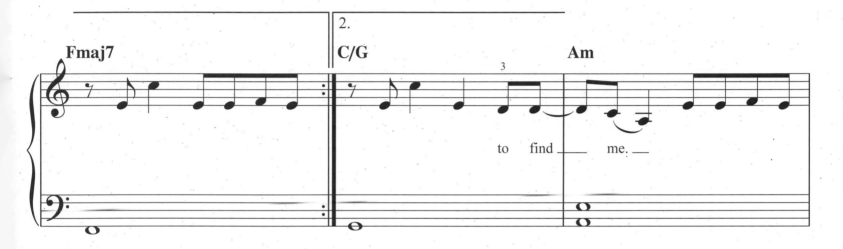

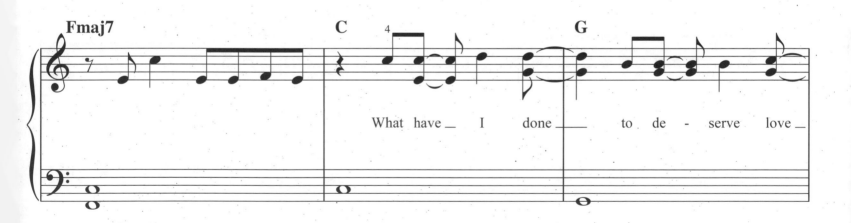

To Coda

G | Am7 | Fmaj7

to de - serve love ___ like ___ this? ___

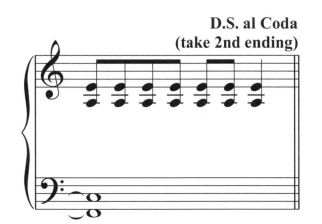

D.S. al Coda
(take 2nd ending)

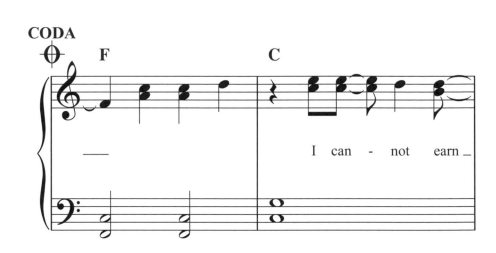

CODA

F | C

___ I can - not earn ___

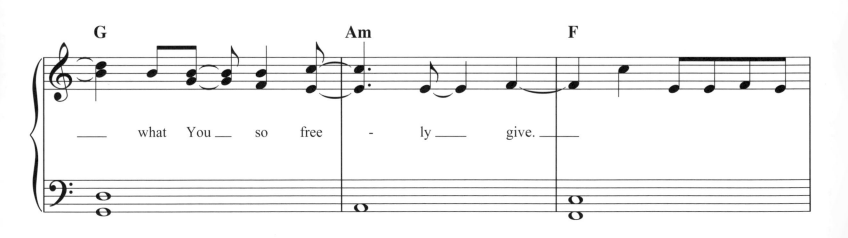

G | Am | F

___ what You ___ so free - ly ___ give. ___

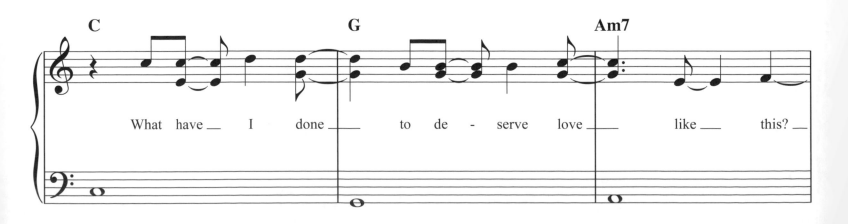

C | G | Am7

What have ___ I done ___ to de - serve love ___ like ___ this?

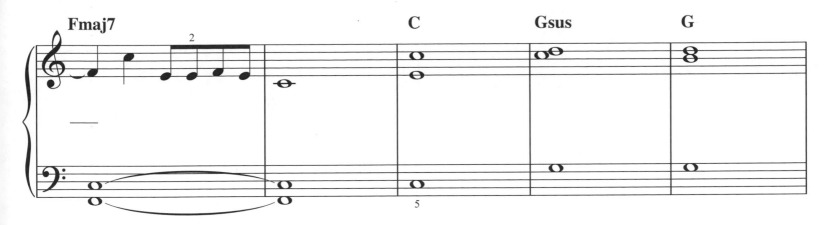

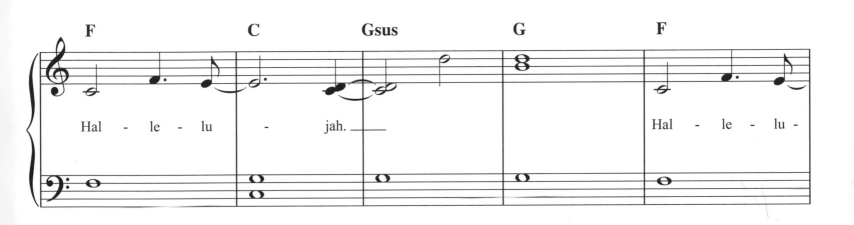

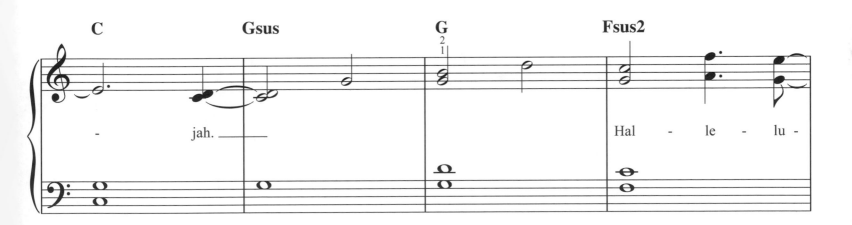

lu - jah. What have _ I done _

_ to de - serve love _ like _ this?

I can - not earn _ what You _ so free - ly _ give. _

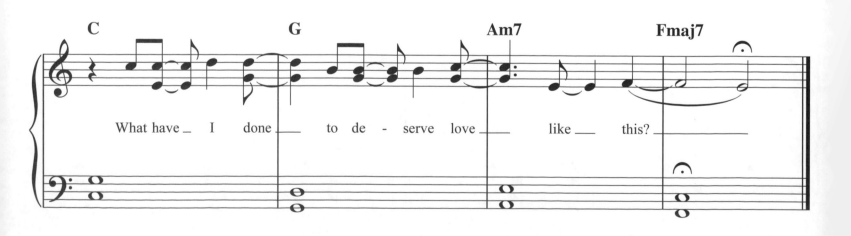

What have _ I done _ to de - serve love _ like _ this?

THIS GIRL

Words and Music by LAUREN DAIGLE,
PAUL DUNCAN, JASON INGRAM
and PAUL MABURY

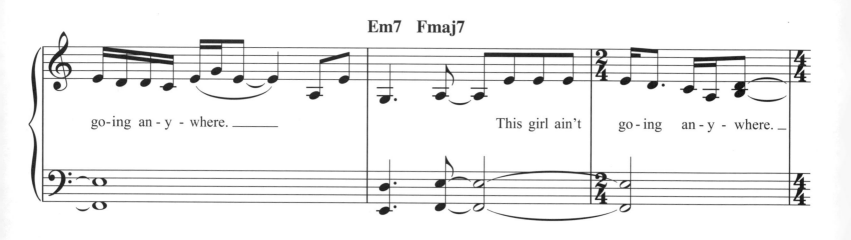

I've searched the world ___ to find all I'm look - ing for.   I want

noth - ing more.   Oh, my heart is Yours. ___

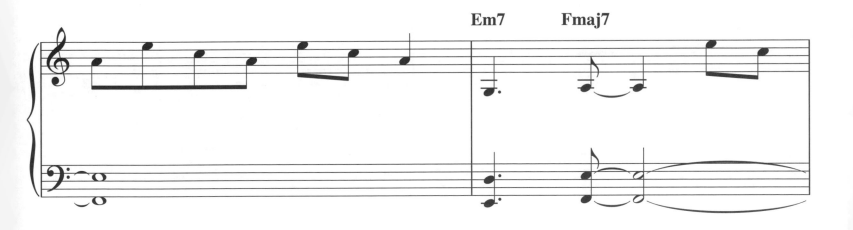

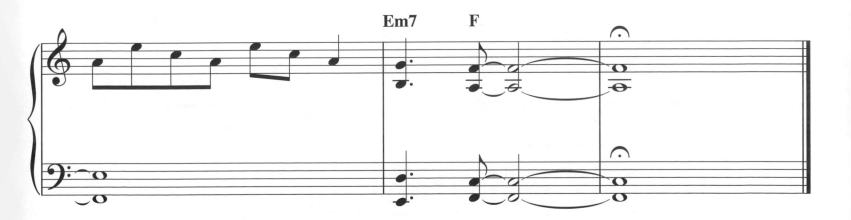

YOUR WINGS

Words and Music by LAUREN DAIGLE,
JASON INGRAM, PAUL MABURY
and LAUREN STRAHM

Moderately slow

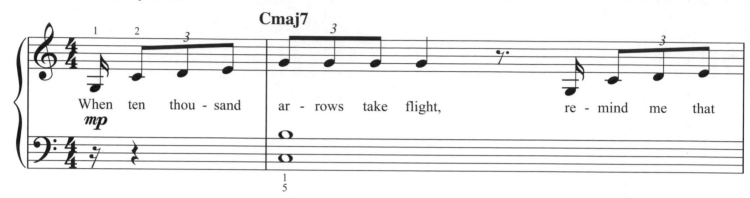

When ten thou-sand ar-rows take flight, re-mind me that

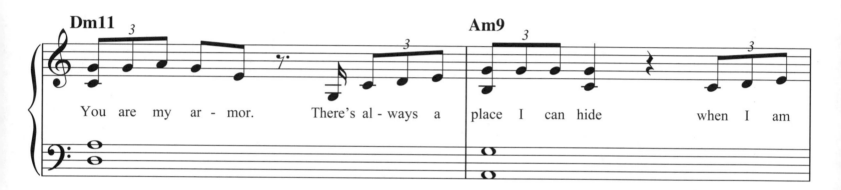

You are my ar-mor. There's al-ways a place I can hide when I am

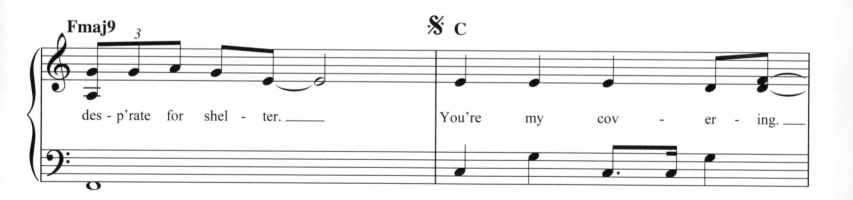

des-p'rate for shel-ter. You're my cov-er-ing.

I'm safe, I'm

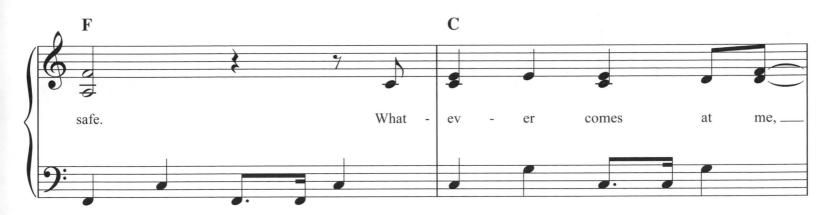

safe. What - ev - er comes at me,

Dm   Am   F

I'm safe, I'm safe. You got me

C   Dm

un - der Your wings, un - der Your wings, I'm un - der, I'm un - der Your wings. You got me.

Am   **To Coda** ⊕ F

You cov - er me, You cov - er me. I'm un - der, I'm un - der Your wings. With ev - 'ry

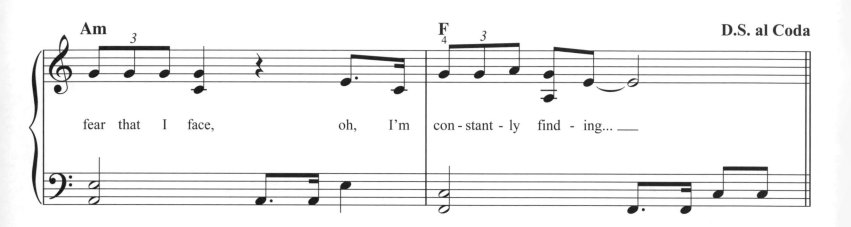

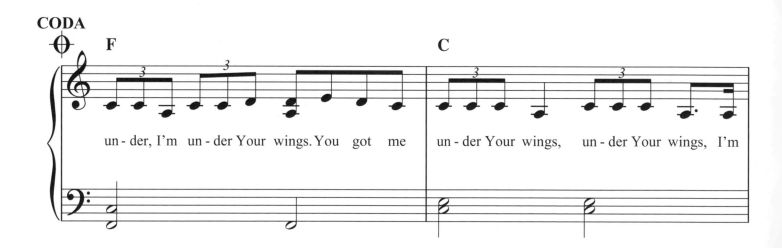

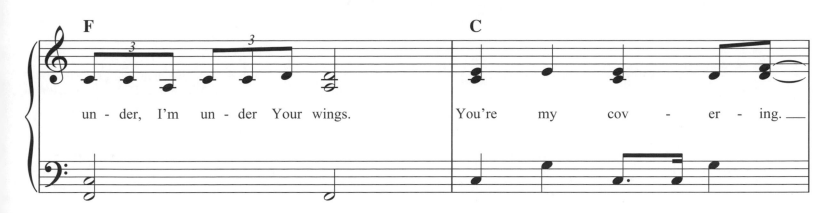

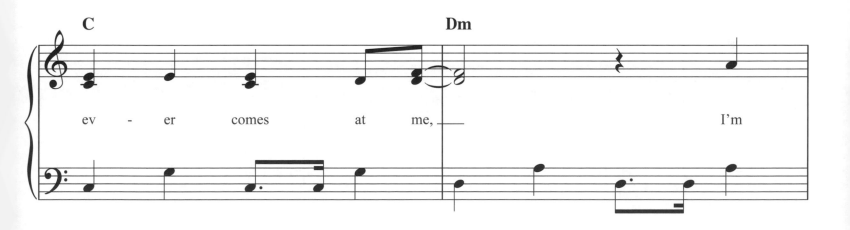

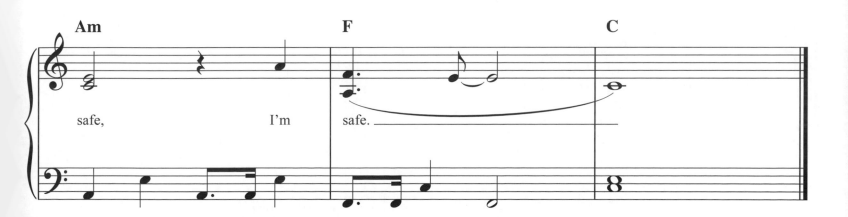

YOU SAY

Words and Music by LAUREN DAIGLE,
JASON INGRAM and PAUL MABURY

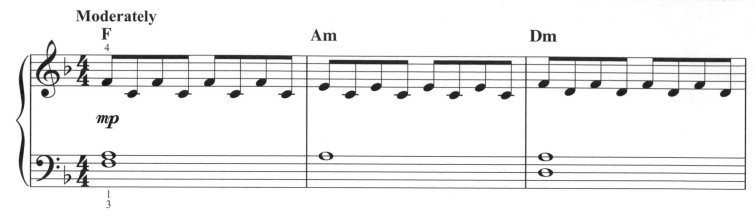

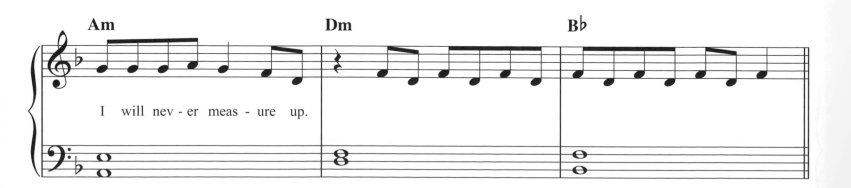

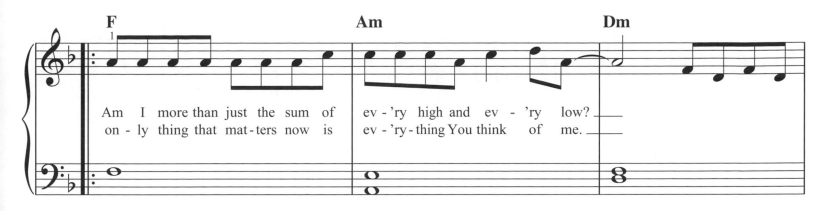

Am I more than just the sum of ev-'ry high and ev-'ry low?
on-ly thing that mat-ters now is ev-'ry-thing You think of me.

Re-mind me once a-gain just who I am, be-cause I need to know.
In You I find my worth, in You I find my i-den-ti-ty.

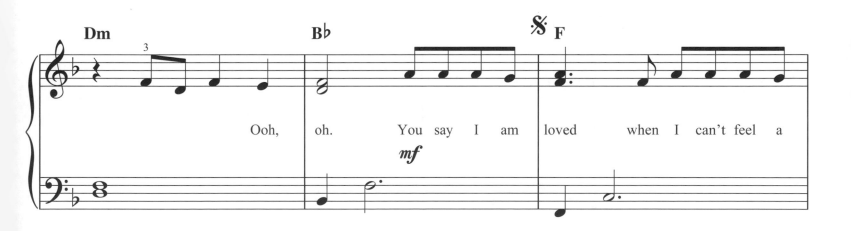

Ooh, oh. You say I am loved when I can't feel a

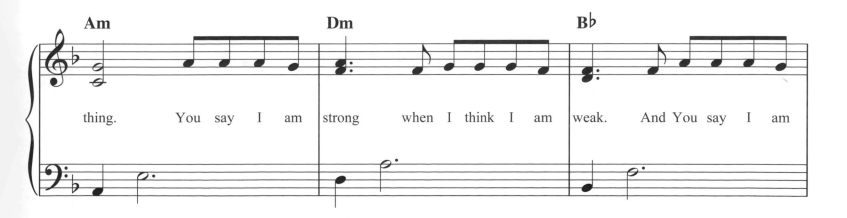

thing. You say I am strong when I think I am weak. And You say I am

held when I am fall - ing short. And when I don't be long, oh, You say I am

To Coda ⊕

Yours, and I be - lieve, oh, I be - lieve what You say of me. I be -

1. lieve. The 2. lieve. Tak-ing all I have, and now I'm

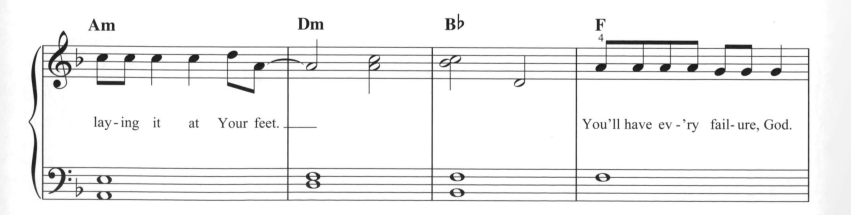

lay-ing it at Your feet. You'll have ev-'ry fail-ure, God.

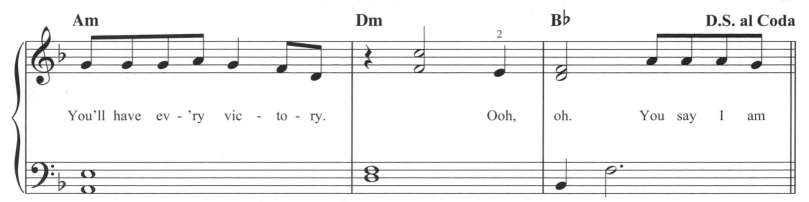

You'll have ev-'ry vic - to - ry.   Ooh,   oh.   You say I am

D.S. al Coda

CODA

lieve.   Oh, I be - lieve.   Yes, I be - lieve   what You say of

me.   I be - lieve.

EVERYTHING

Words and Music by LAUREN DAIGLE,
JASON INGRAM and PAUL MABURY

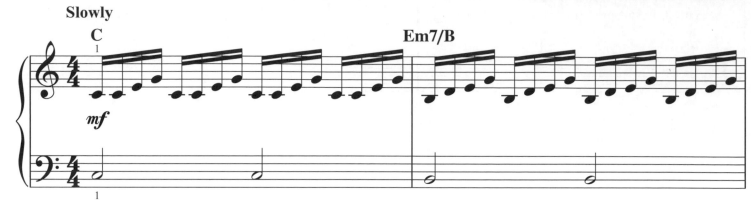

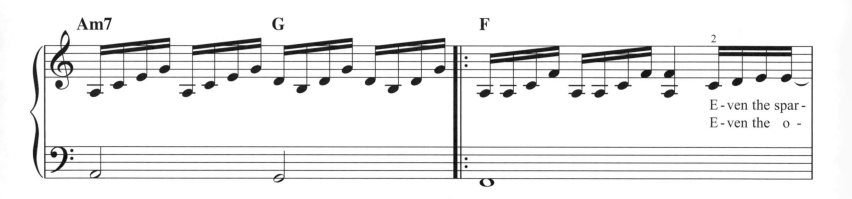

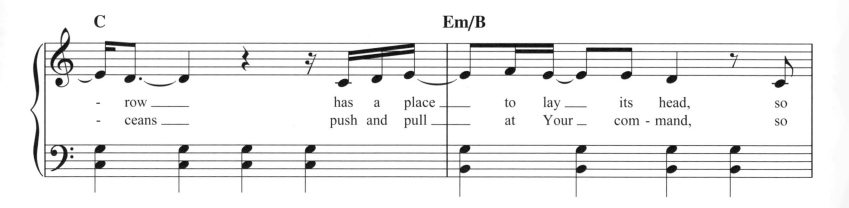

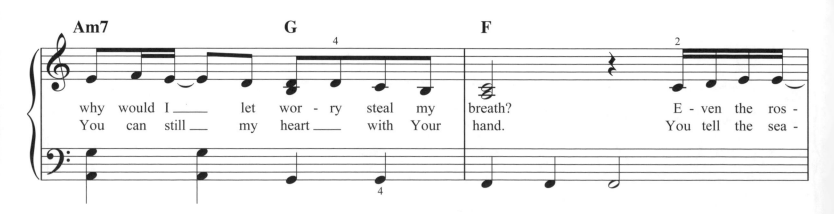

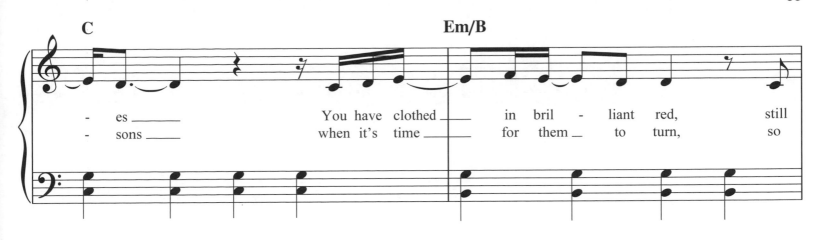

C   Em/B

- es _____   You have clothed _____   in bril - liant red,   still
- sons _____   when it's time _____   for them __ to turn,   so

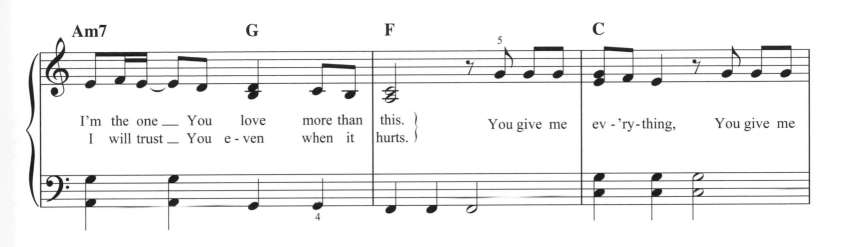

Am7   G   F   C

I'm the one __ You   love   more than this.   You give me   ev -'ry-thing,   You give me
I will trust __ You e - ven   when it   hurts.

Em/B   Am7   1.

F

ev - 'ry - thing,   You give me   ev - 'ry - thing   I _____ need.

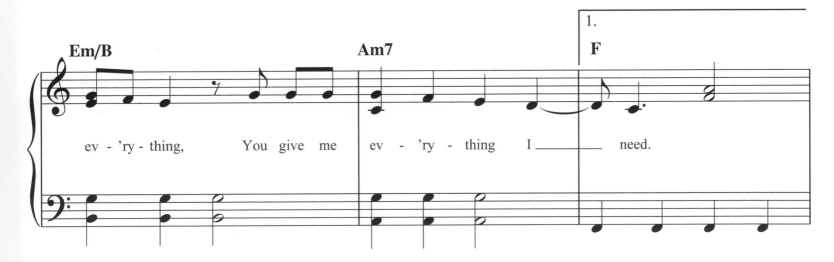

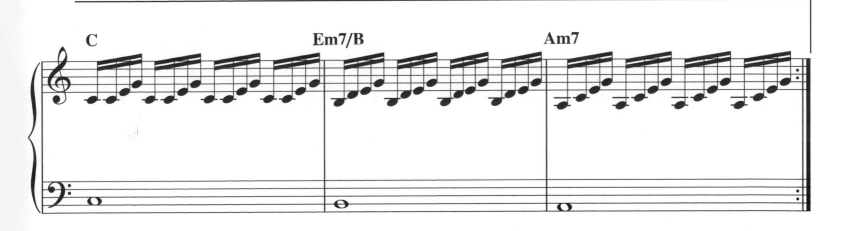

C   Em7/B   Am7

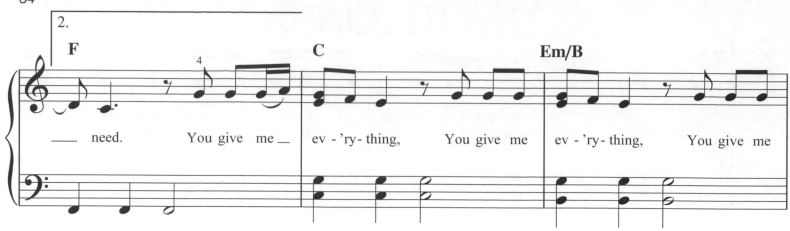

need. You give me __ ev-'ry-thing, You give me ev-'ry-thing, You give me

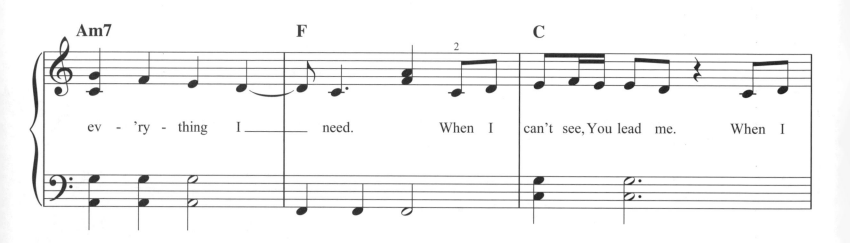

ev - 'ry - thing I _____ need. When I can't see, You lead me. When I

can't hear, You show me. When I can't stand, You car - ry me. ___ When I'm

lost, You will find me. When I'm weak, You are might - y. You are

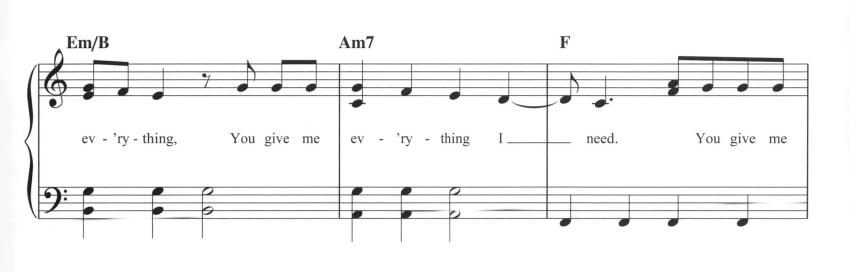

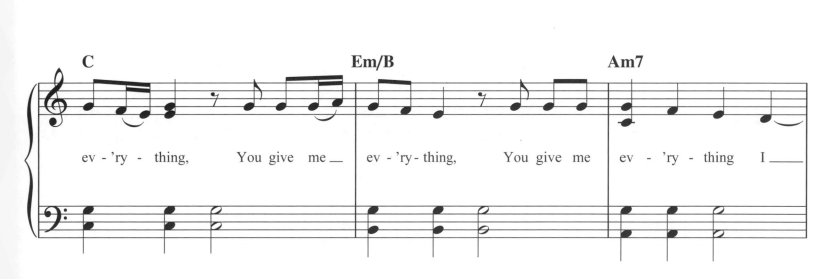

LOOK UP CHILD

Words and Music by LAUREN DAIGLE,
JASON INGRAM and PAUL MABURY

I hear You say, ___ I hear You say, ___ "Look up, child, ___

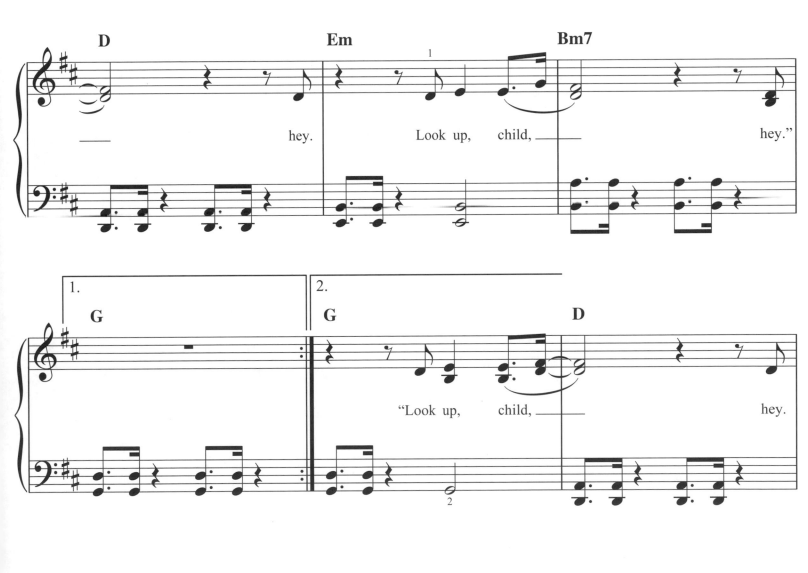

___ hey. Look up, child, ___ hey."

1.

2.

"Look up, child, ___ hey.

Look up, child, ___ hey. Look up." You're not

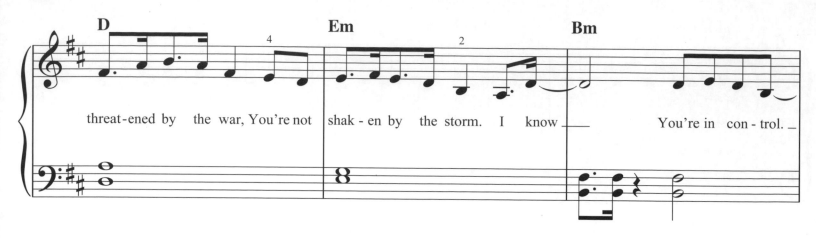

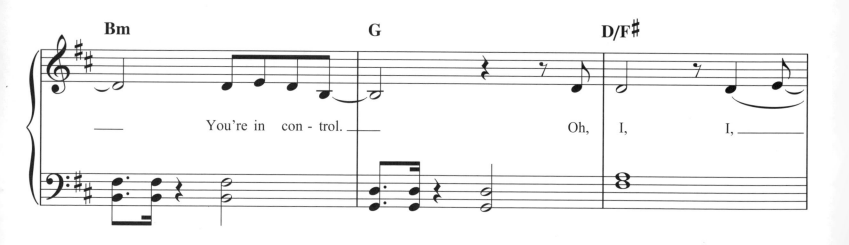

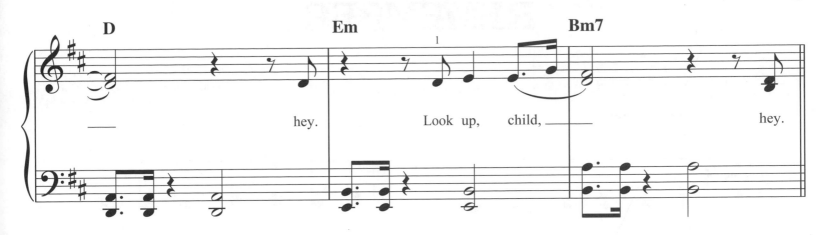

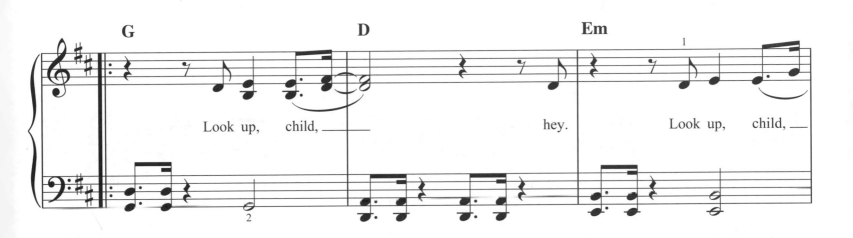

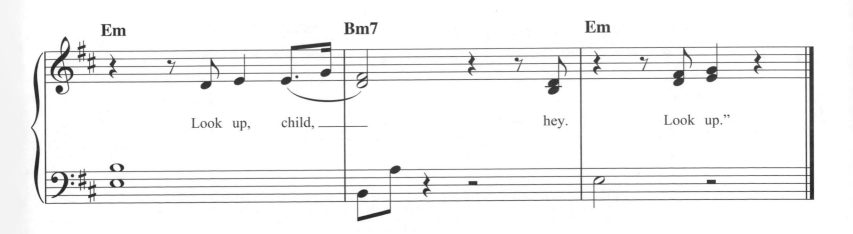

REMEMBER

Words and Music by LAUREN DAIGLE,
CHRIS TOMLIN, JASON INGRAM
and PAUL MABURY

In the dark-est ___ ho-ur, when I can-not ___ breathe,
I will lift my ___ eyes, e-ven in the ___ pain.

fear is on my chest, the weight of the world on __ me.
A-bove all the lies, I know You can make a way.

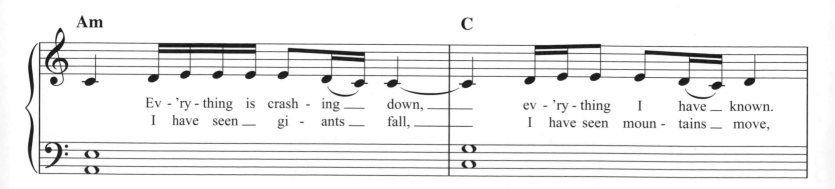

Ev-'ry-thing is crash-ing ___ down, ___ ev-'ry-thing I have __ known.
I have seen __ gi-ants __ fall, ___ I have seen moun-tains __ move,

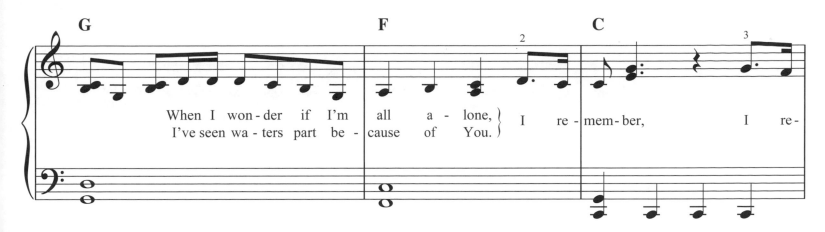

G   F   C

When I won-der if I'm all a - lone,
I've seen wa-ters part be - cause of You. I re - mem-ber, I re-

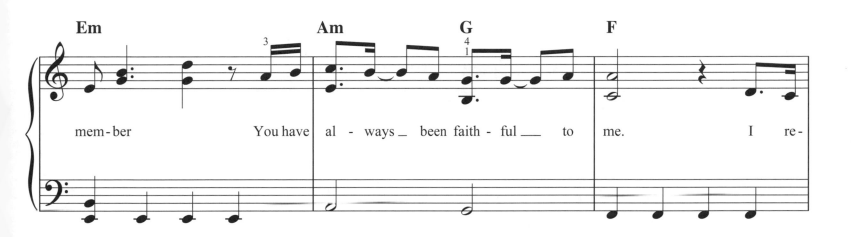

Em   Am   G   F

mem-ber You have al - ways __ been faith - ful __ to me. I re-

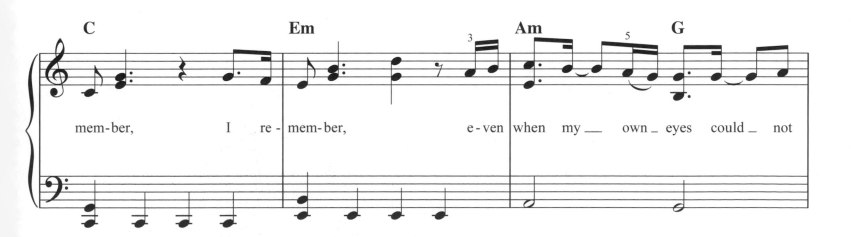

C   Em   Am   G

mem-ber, I re - mem-ber, e - ven when my __ own __ eyes could __ not

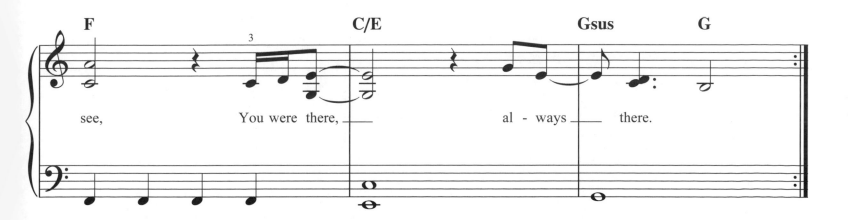

F   C/E   Gsus   G

see, You were there, __ al - ways __ there.

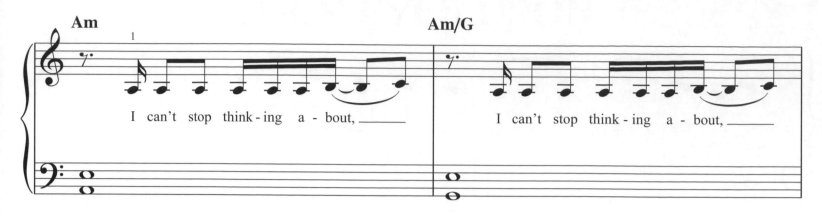

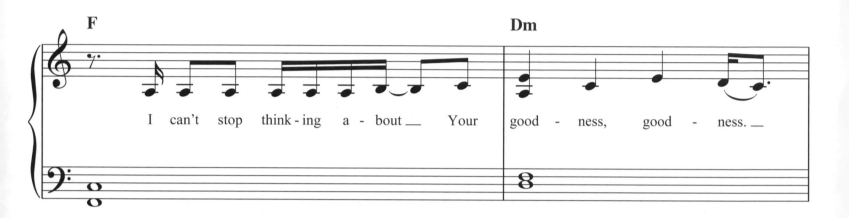

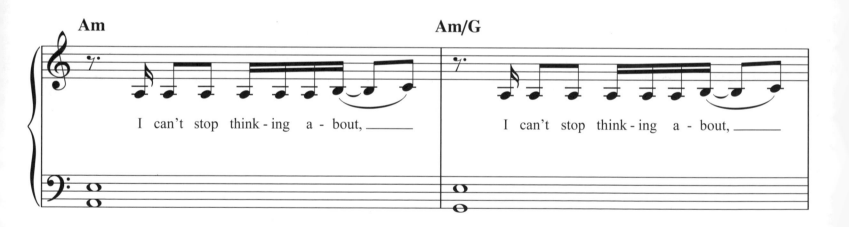

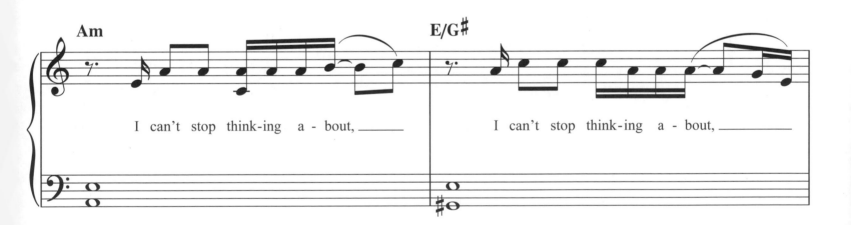

C   Em   Am   G

mem - ber,   I re - mem - ber _____   You have al - ways __ been faith - ful __ to

F   C   Em   3

me.   I re - mem - ber,   I re - mem - ber,   e - ven

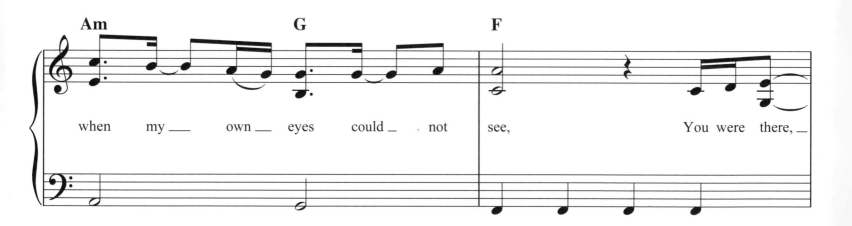

Am   G   F

when my __ own __ eyes   could __ not   see,   You were there, __

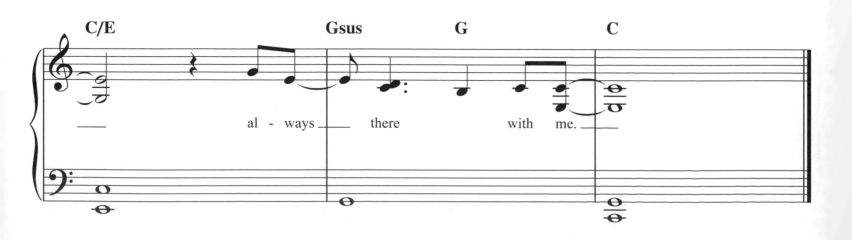

C/E   Gsus   G   C

__   al - ways __ there   with me. __

LOSING MY RELIGION

Words and Music by LAUREN DAIGLE,
JASON INGRAM and PAUL MABURY

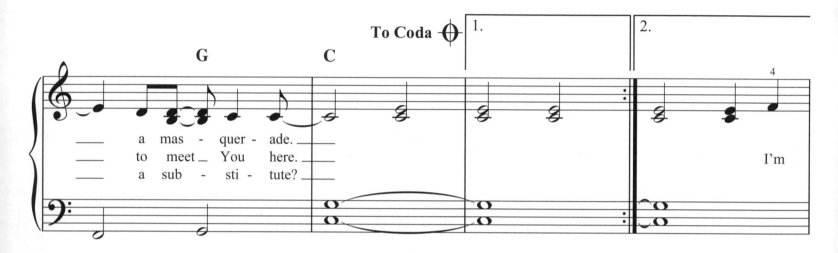

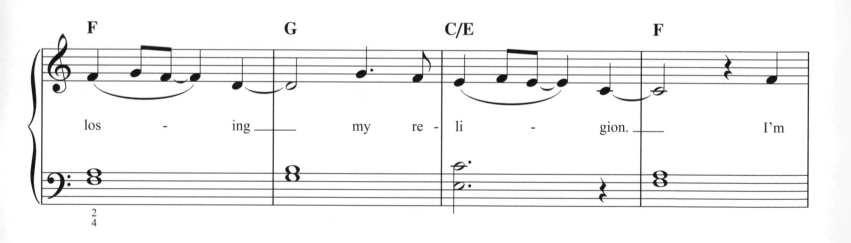

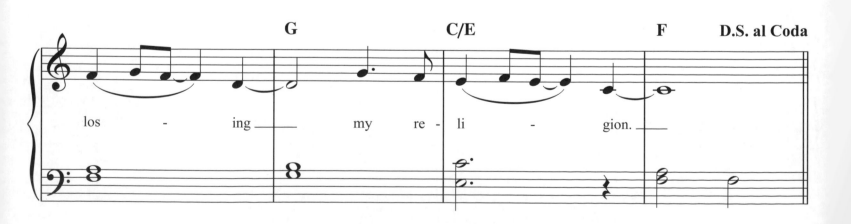

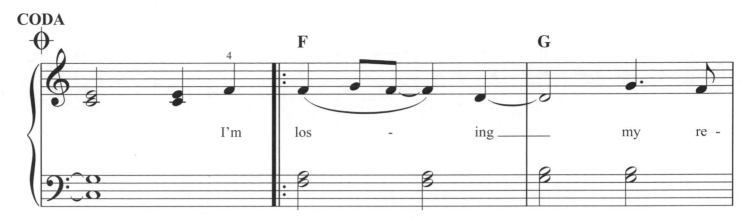

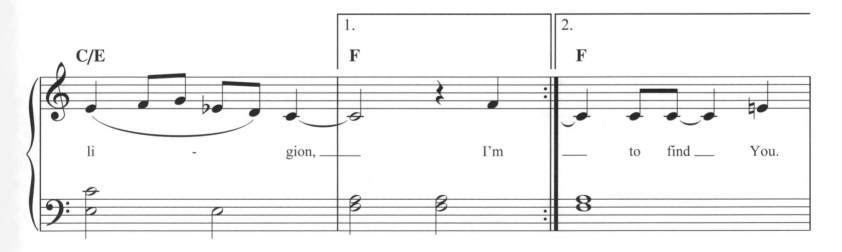

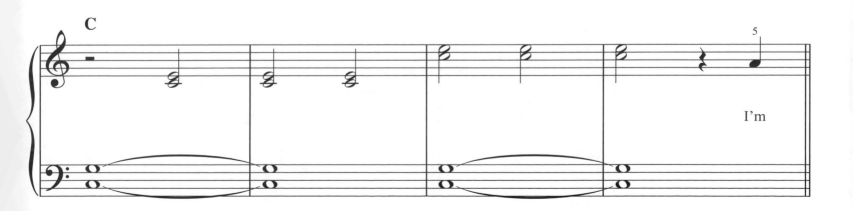

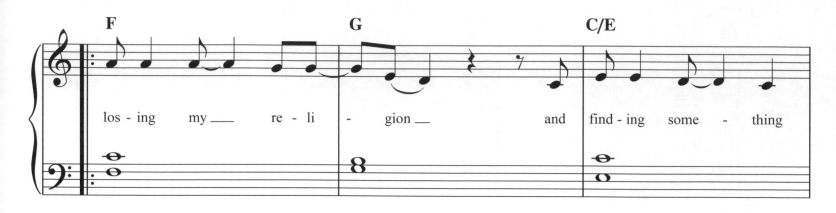

los - ing my ___ re - li - gion ___ and find - ing some - thing

new. 'Cause I need some - thing dif - f'rent, ___ and

dif-f'rent looks ___ like You. I'm You.

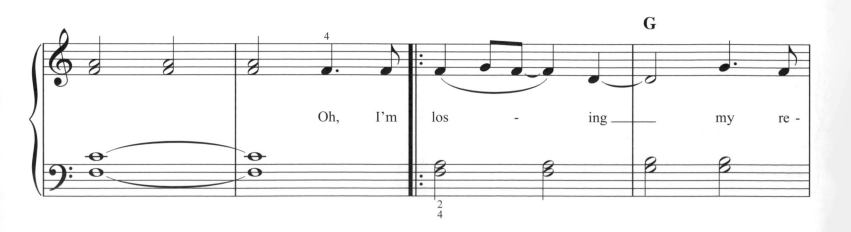

Oh, I'm los - ing ___ my re-

REBEL HEART

Words and Music by LAUREN DAIGLE,
PAUL DUNCAN and PAUL MABURY

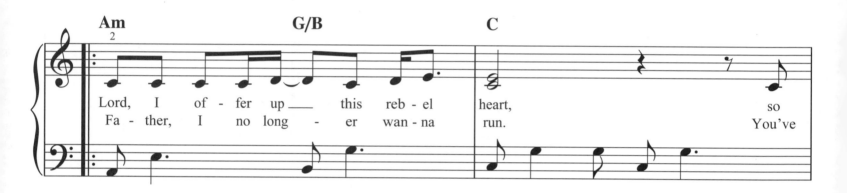

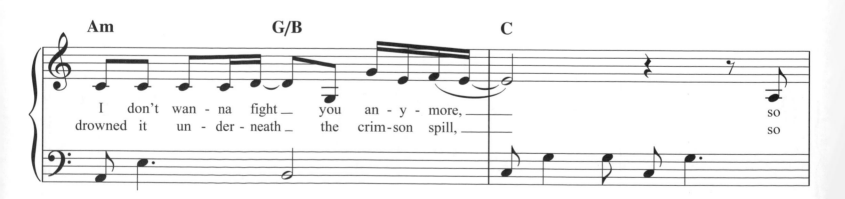

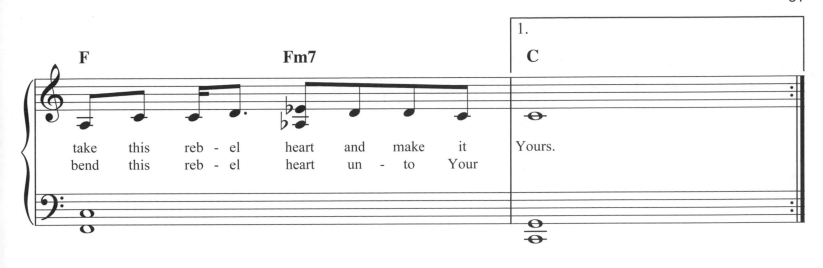

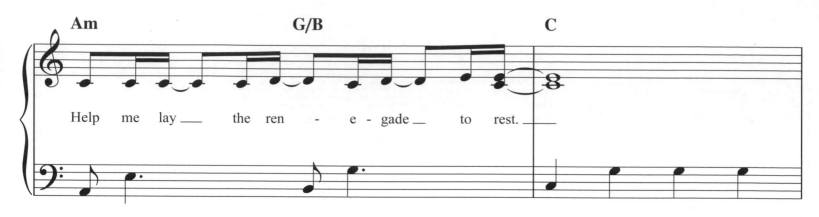

Help me lay ___ the ren - e - gade ___ to rest. ___

Turn the stone ___ in - side ___ me back ___ to flesh. ___ And

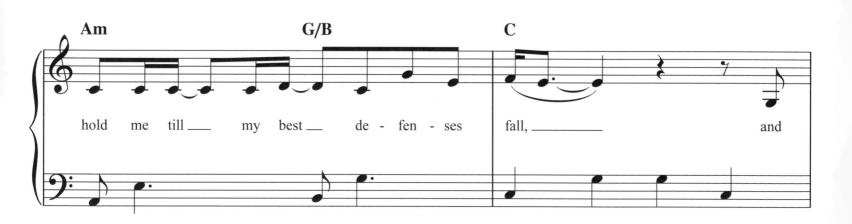

hold me till ___ my best ___ de - fen - ses fall, _____ and

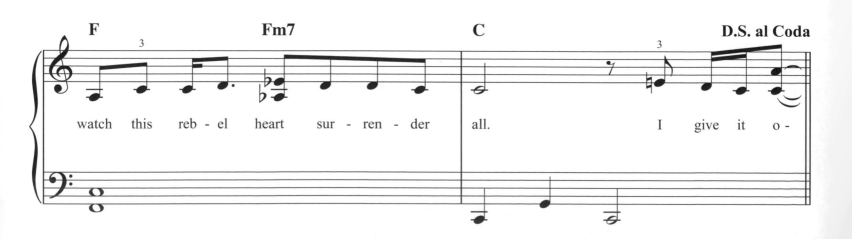

watch this reb - el heart sur - ren - der all. I give it o-

CODA

You. Oh, take my life and let it be _____ Yours. _____

_____ Oh, take my life and let it be _____ Yours. _____ Oh, _____

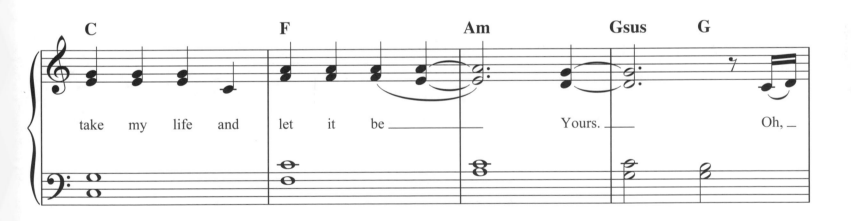

take my life and let it be _____ Yours. _____ Oh, _____

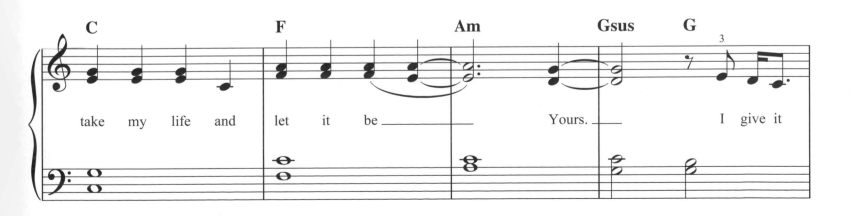

take my life and let it be _____ Yours. _____ I give it

54

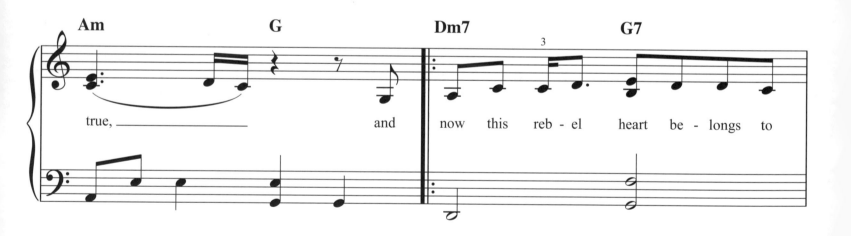

INEVITABLE

Words and Music by LAUREN DAIGLE,
PAUL DUNCAN and PAUL MABURY

Ev - er run - ning to what I can't ____ see,

fight - ing out of all my un - be - lief.

Fa - ther, e - ven then, my song will ____ be: ____

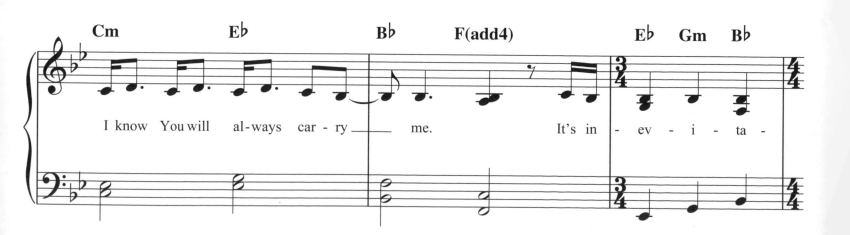

I know You will al - ways car - ry ____ me. It's in - ev - i - ta -

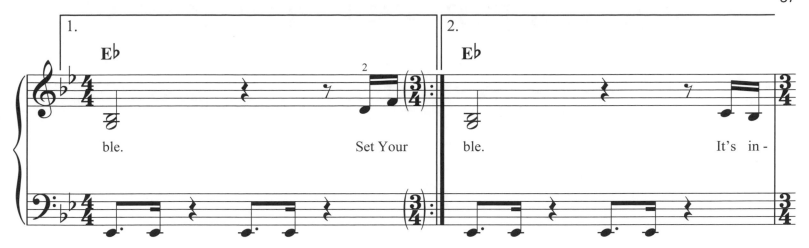

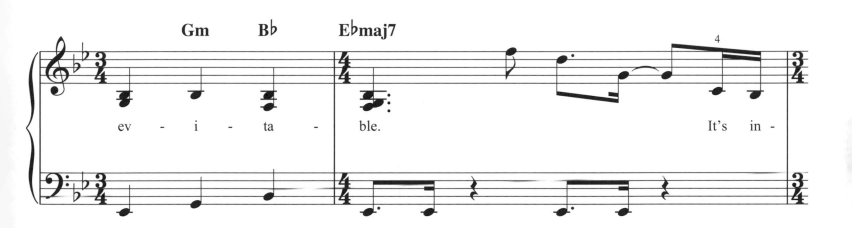

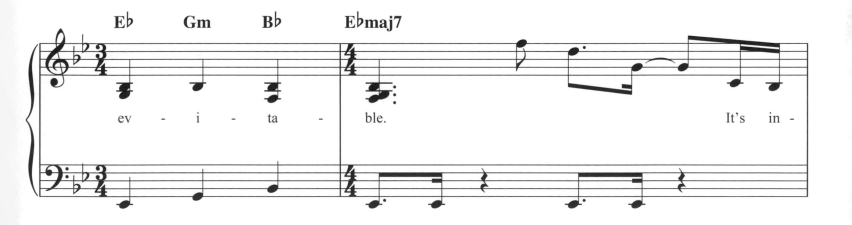

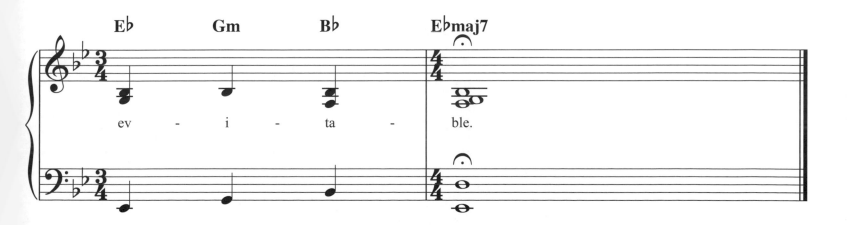

TURN YOUR EYES UPON JESUS

Words and Music by LAUREN DAIGLE,
DWAN HILL and PAUL MABURY

Moderately slow, relaxed feel

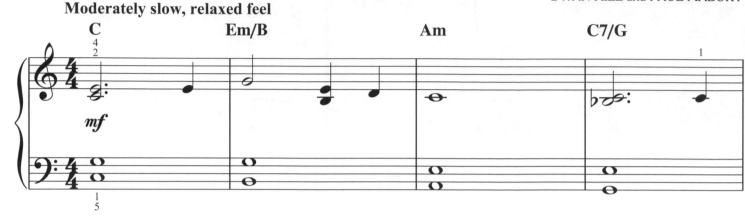

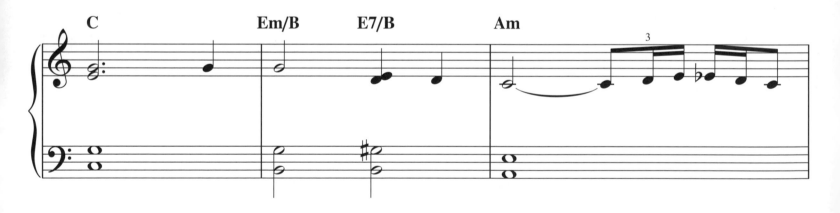

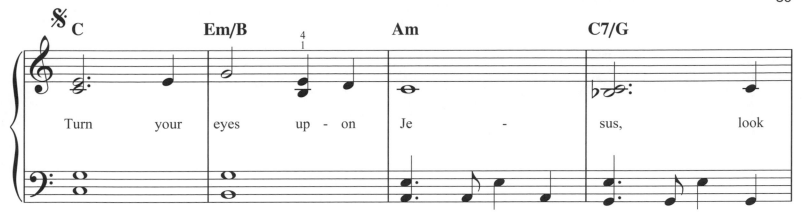

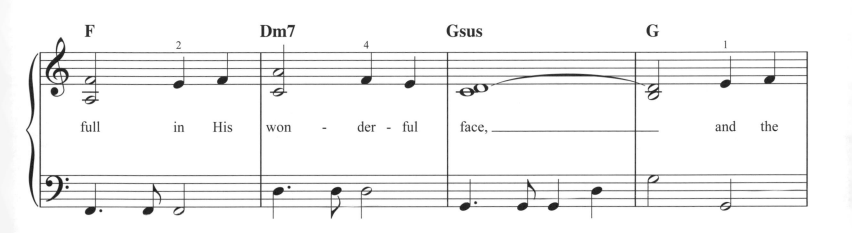

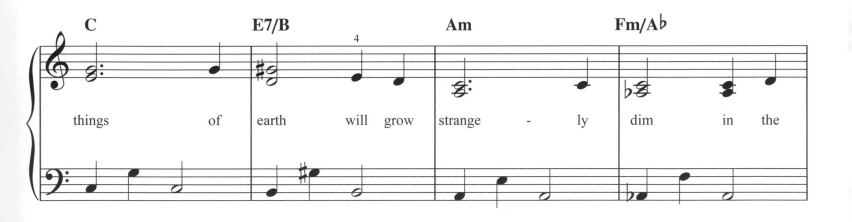

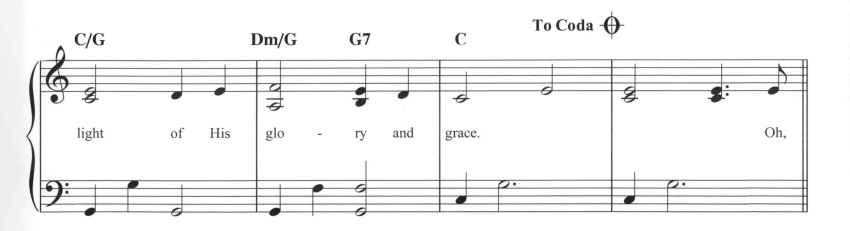

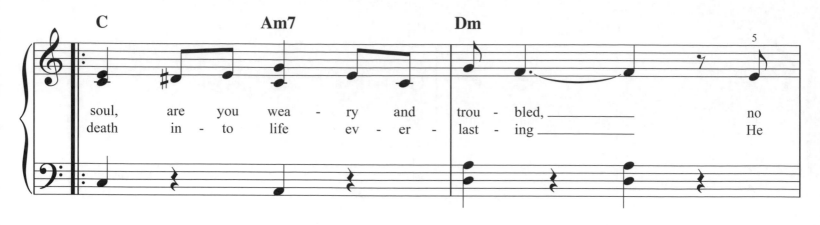

C **Am7** **Dm**

soul, are you wea - ry and trou - bled, _____ no
death in - to life ev - er - last - ing _____ He

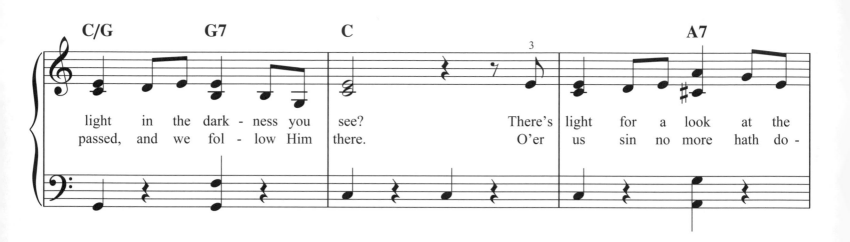

C/G **G7** **C** **A7**

light in the dark - ness you see? There's light for a look at the
passed, and we fol - low Him there. O'er us sin no more hath do -

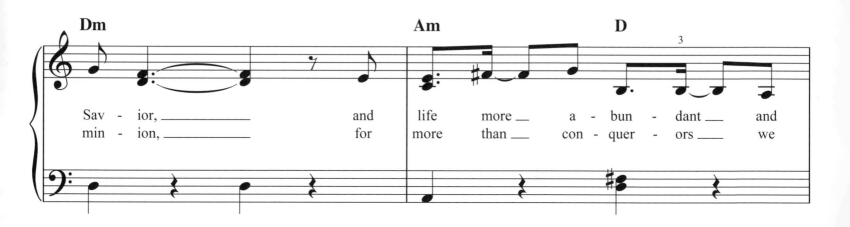

Dm **Am** **D**

Sav - ior, _____ and life more __ a - bun - dant __ and
min - ion, _____ for more than __ con - quer - ors __ we

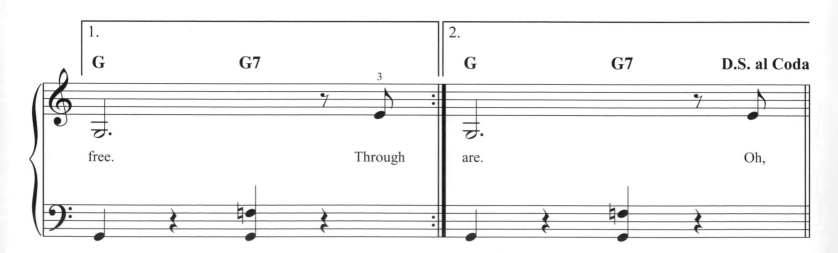

1. **G** **G7** | 2. **G** **G7** **D.S. al Coda**

free. Through | are. Oh,

CODA

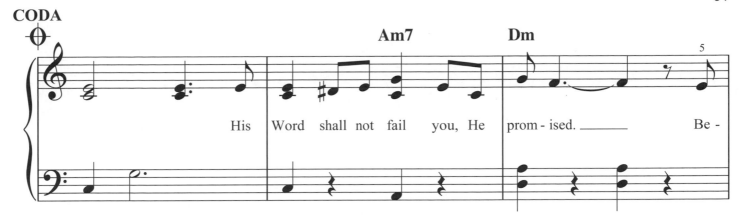

Am7   **Dm**

His Word shall not fail you, He prom - ised. _____ Be -

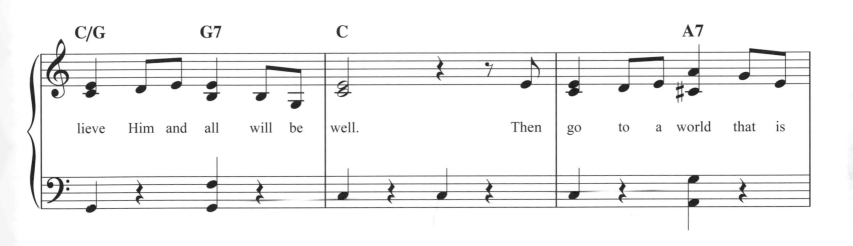

C/G   **G7**   **C**   **A7**

lieve Him and all will be well. Then go to a world that is

Dm   **Am**   **D**   **G**   **G7**

dy - ing, _____ His per - fect _ sal - va - tion _ to tell. Oh,

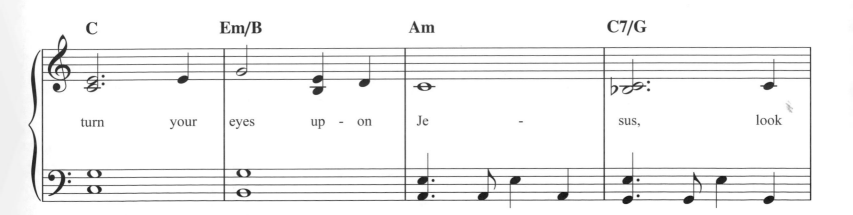

C   **Em/B**   **Am**   **C7/G**

turn your eyes up - on Je - sus, look

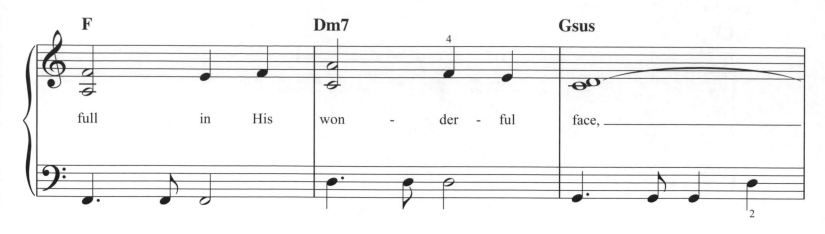

F   **Dm7**   **Gsus**

full   in His   won - der - ful   face, _____

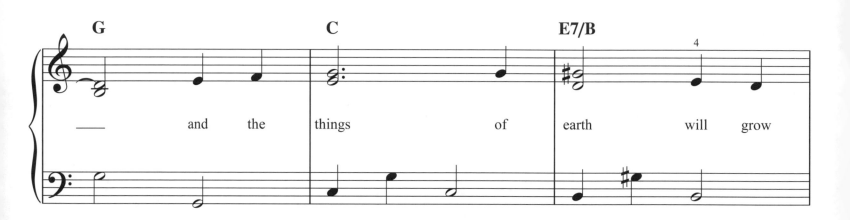

G   **C**   **E7/B**

___   and the   things   of   earth   will   grow

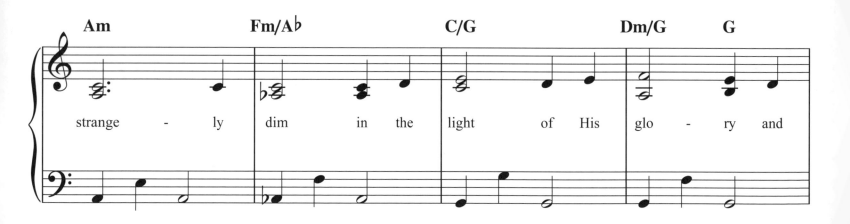

Am   **Fm/A♭**   **C/G**   **Dm/G**   **G**

strange - ly   dim   in the   light   of His   glo - ry and

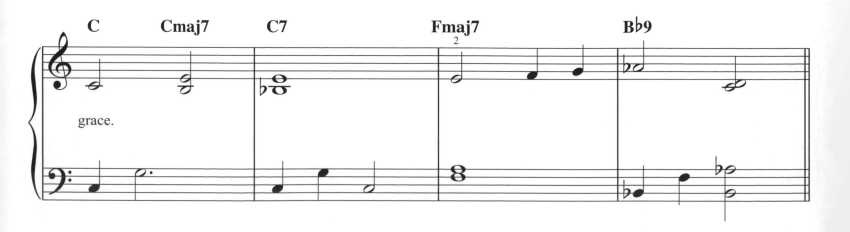

C   **Cmaj7**   **C7**   **Fmaj7**   **B♭9**

grace.

Oh, turn your, _ oh, turn your, _ oh turn your _ eyes u-pon Je - sus.

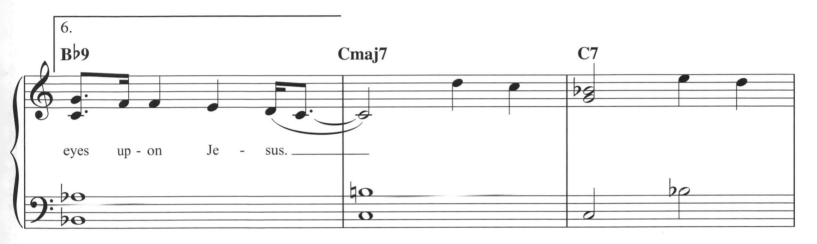

eyes up-on Je - sus. _

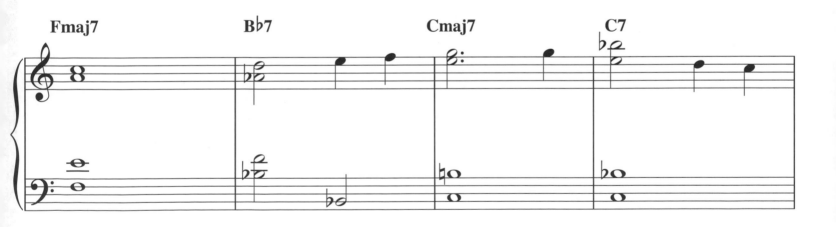

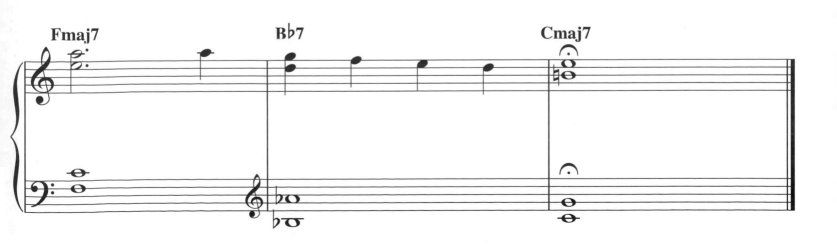